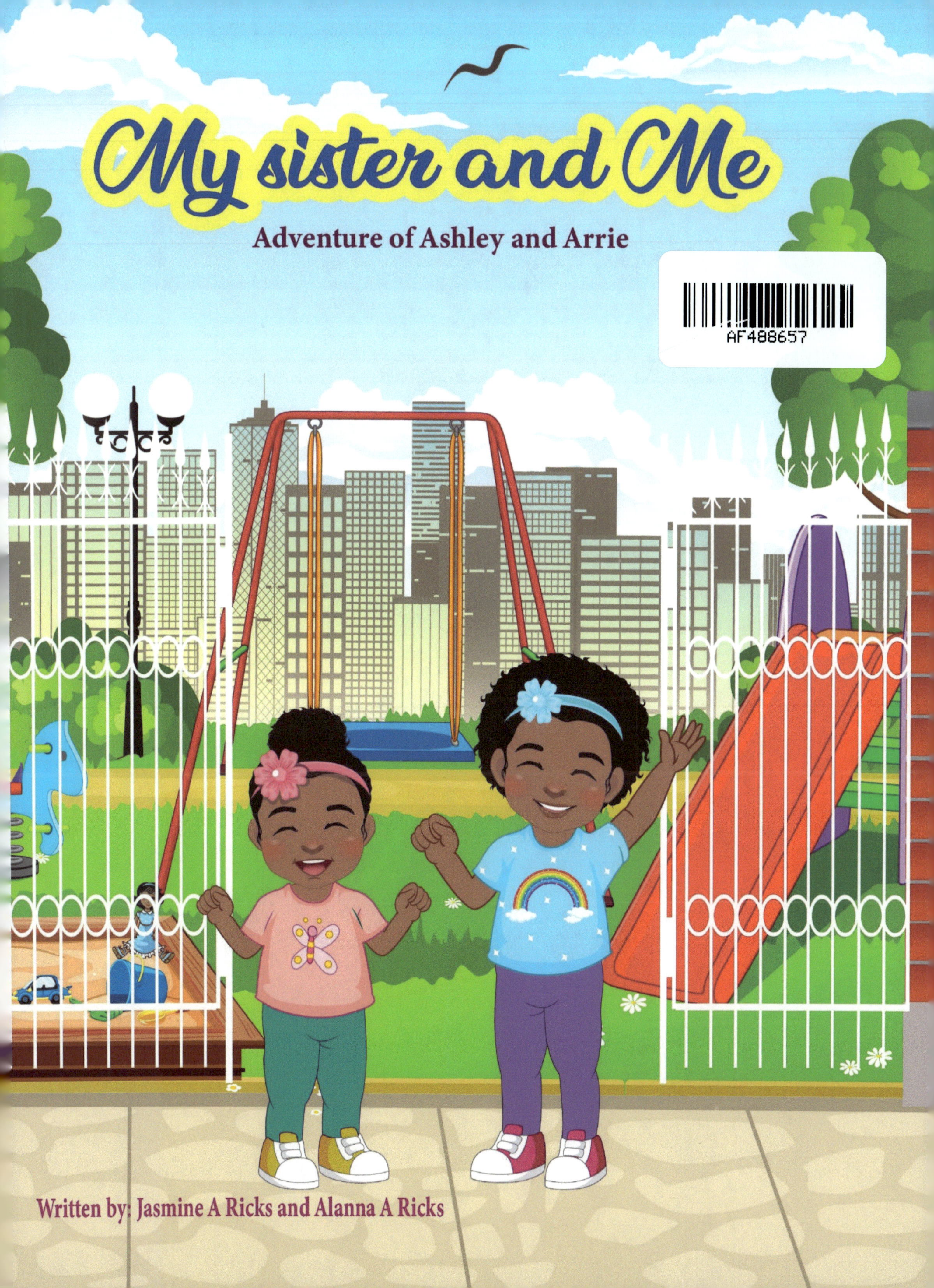

My sister and Me
Adventure of Ashley and Arrie
AF488657
Written by: Jasmine A Ricks and Alanna A Ricks

This book is dedicated to

Mrs. Holmes of the House of Smiles
Mrs. Jackson Of Berkely Citizens
Mrs. McHenry
Mrs. Forster of Head Start
And all apart of Jasmine and Alanna's team

ISBN - 979-8-9882033-1-5

The sun is shining and the birds sing.
It's morning time. Let's start the day.

Where is mom taking us today?

Mom, can we go to school? Shopping!
The park to play?

Sorry girls, it's Saturday, it's the weekend. Time for laughter and play. What do you two want to do today.

Help mommy cook breakfast. Ingredients!!!! Pancake mix, water, eggs, and sausage.
Pour 1 cup of pancake mix
1/2 cup of water
3 eggs
Annnnd Mix it together

Yummy yummy breakfast!! So sweet and delicious.

But before we can play we help mommy clean
the kitchen.
Ashley clears the table and Arrie wipes the table.
Mommy washes dishes. Bubbles everywhere.

We pop the bubbles. We eat the bubbles,
we stomp the bubbles.
Teamwork can be so fun and full of laughter.

Breakfast is done. Dishes are clean. Mommy mommy what are we doing to day? Where are you taking us?

How about shopping and playing at the park?
We just want to play all day.

To the park it is. To the park it is.
Come on girls come on.

We climb up the slides and slide down the slides.
We swing on the swings.
We fly so high.
We are superheroes.
Weee weeeee weeeee What fun!!!

We play in the sandbox looking for treasure.
We found a small rock, two blue cars, and two
toy dolls.

We play with our baby dolls. We build castles
for our baby dolls hiding them for the dragons.

Arrie!!! Arrie!!! Look!! Two sea dragons
are swimming towards us.

OH NO!!! We will save you dollies!!!

Ashley, duck the dragons are coming towards us..

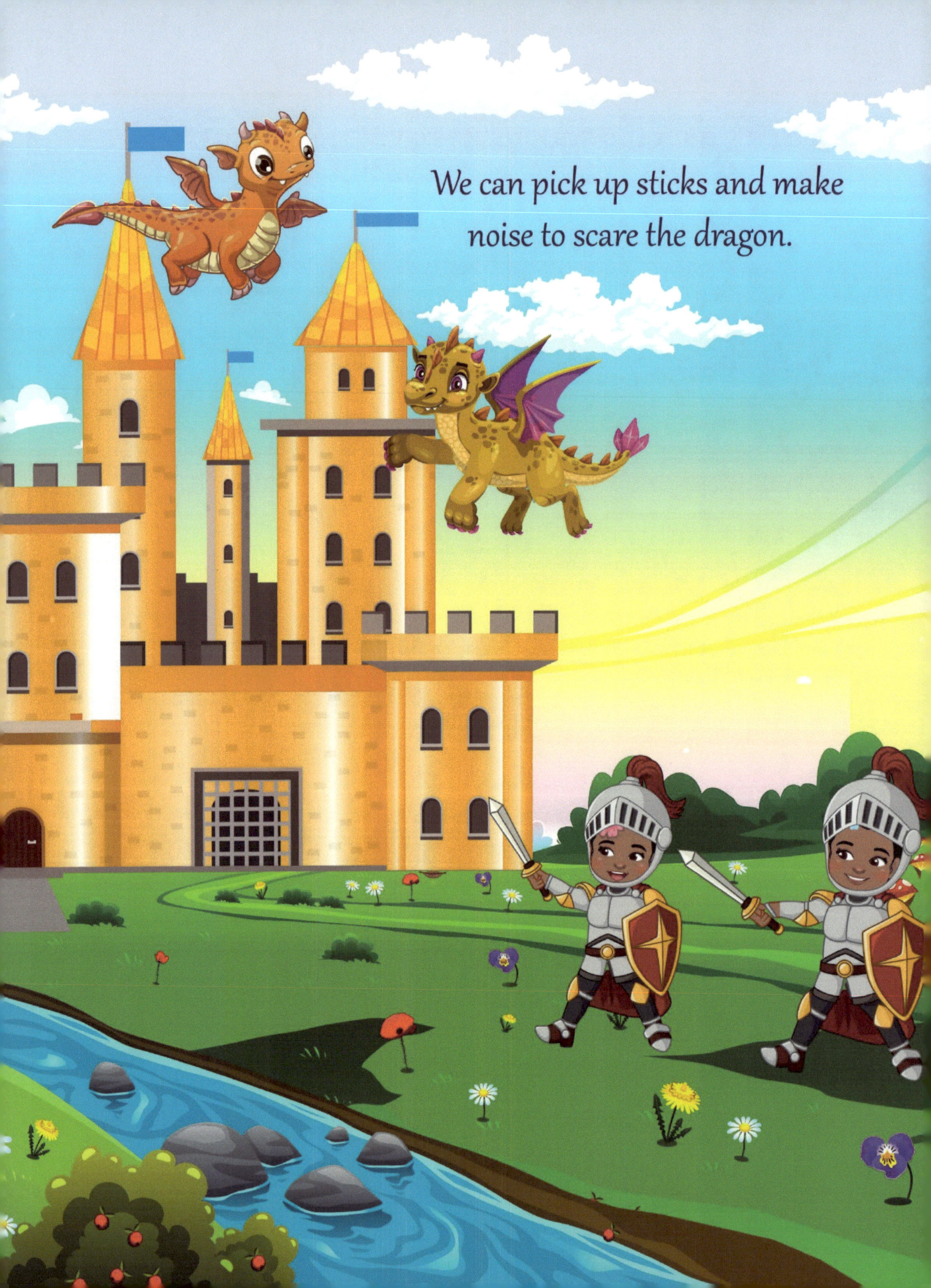

We can pick up sticks and make noise to scare the dragon.

Are you ready? Ashley asked
Arrie. Charge!!!! YAY!! We win
the dragon leaves.

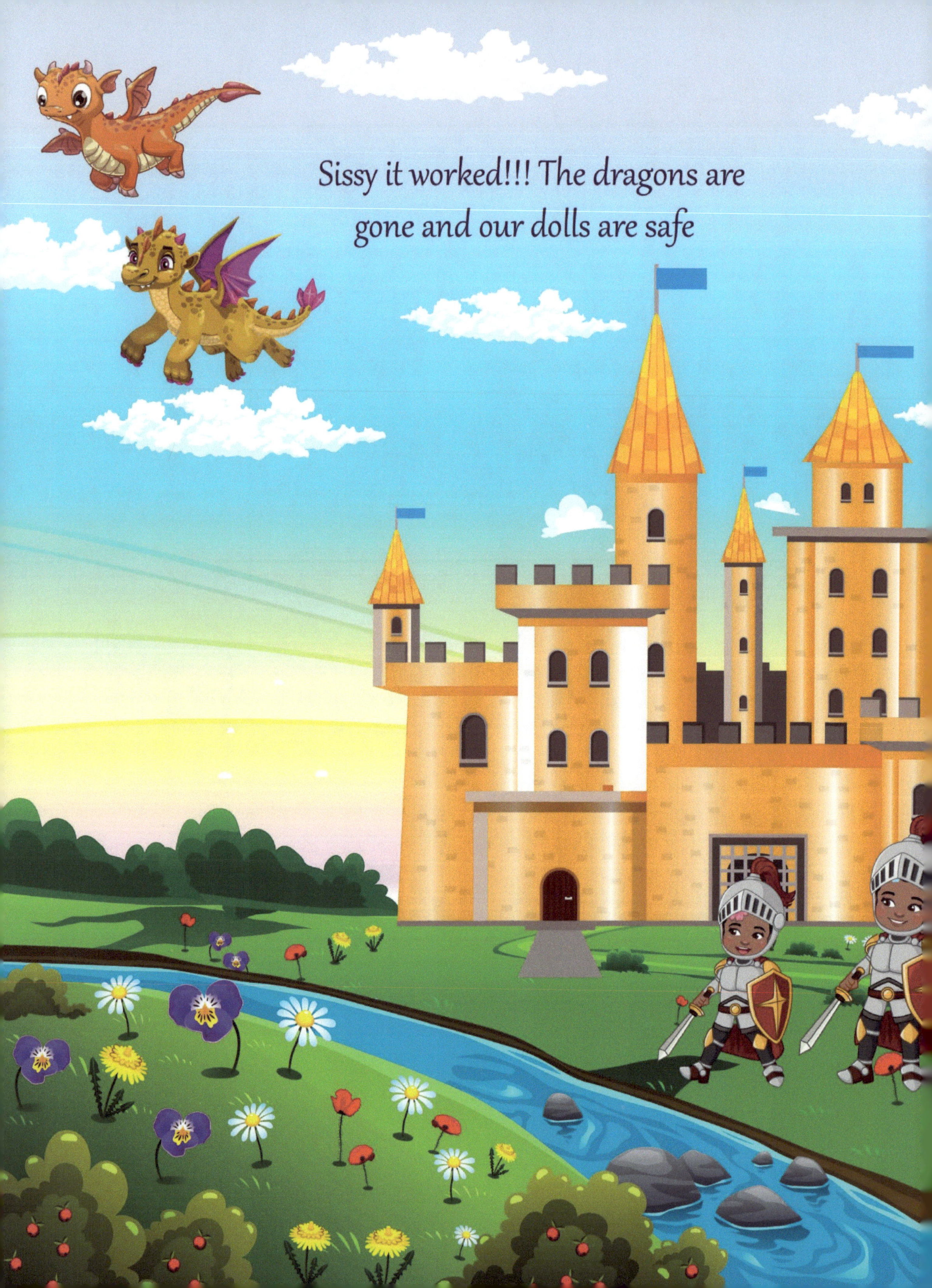

Sissy it worked!!! The dragons are gone and our dolls are safe

Ashley and Arrie it's time
to go. Mommy called

But, But mom, do we have to go? We want to play all day. We want to play in the sun. We want to play with each other. Can we stay???

No girls, it's time to go. We can come back tomorrow.

Mommy we had soooo much
fun today fighting . Thank you!!

I am glad you two had so much fun.
mommy can we come back
tomorrow? Yes, we can my loves.